TURBOCHARGE YOUR GRANNY

TURBOCHARGE YOUR GRANNY

Annie Tempest and Stephen James

MULLER, BLOND & WHITE

First published in Great Britain in 1985 by Muller, Blond & White,
55 Great Ormond Street, London WC1N 3HZ.

British Library Cataloguing in Publication Data

James, Stephen
    Turbocharge your granny.
    1. English wit and humour, Pictorial
    I. Title   II. Tempest, Annie
    741.5'942   NC 1479

ISBN 0 584 11127 4

Printed and bound in Great Britain by
R. J. Acford, Industrial Estate, Chichester, Sussex

to
Piers,
Putney Hospital,
melanie, Susie
and
Grannies
everywhere

Dear Reader

There are seven million Grannies alive and kicking in England today. Yes, SEVEN MILLION! In a few years time we'll be swamped, awash with blue rinses, snowed under with curlers. It'll be standing room only on all Inter City 125s. There won't be a can of prunes left.

And that's just England. Think how many Grannies there are tucked away in Scotland, lurking in Ireland, hidden at a secret address in Wales, or the United States . . . or Japan!

Like plants, Grannies need looking after. Regular feeding (essential in winter), a stable temperature, and plenty of sunlight. Talked to, Grannies flourish. Left alone and unloved, they grow wild.

This little book is for all those in Life's Garden who care. It's packed full of ideas to get Granny going, and going, until she's gone! Faster wheelchairs! Stronger reinforced stockings! Cheaper winter holidays! Hotter meals on wheels!

So get to it. Go TURBOCHARGE YOUR GRANNY!

Annie and *Stephen*

...and for all Grannies who can't quite read the small print:

DEAR GRANNY,
THIS LITTLE BOOK IS ESPECIALLY FOR YOU!

If she starts to nod off...

stoke up her fire.

If she can't get to sleep...

mix her a nightcap.

If she can't get out of bed in the morning . . .

mend her teasmade.

Dead-head her roses.

Redesign her rockery.

If her cuttings won't take...

rent her a nice allotment.

Take her shopping.

Collect her pension.

Recharge her hearing aid.

Teach her the Green Cross Code.

Motorize her flying ducks.

If she loses her patience . . .

play bridge with her.

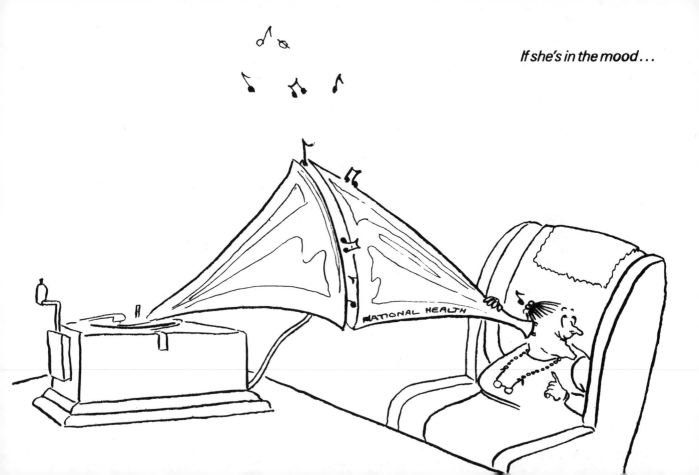

take her dancing.

Make her feel nostalgic.

Ensure she gets regular exercise.

Bring her to the local fete . . .

and see if she likes coconuts.

If Granny gets hungry...

speed up her meals on wheels.

If she starts to peg out . . .

give her plenty of iron.

If F-Plan's not her plan...

try her on G-Plan.

If she gets tired of hanging around ...

send her sightseeing.

Amuse her.

Send her on Safari.

If Granny wants to get out and about...

turbocharge her wheelchair.

Introduce her to your friends . . .

and take her to tea with hers.

Trim her moustache.

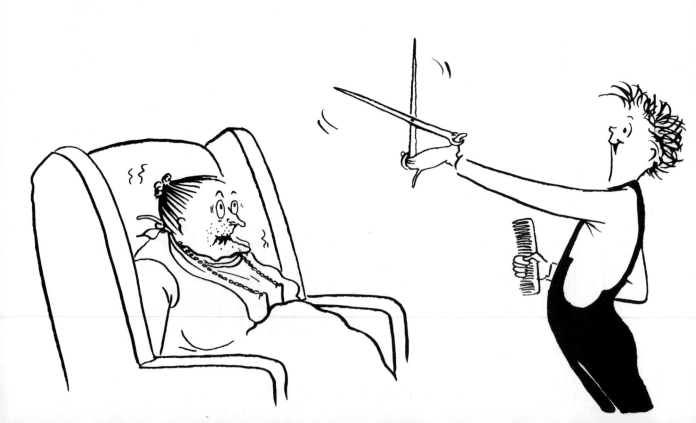

IN GRANNYCARE

Clean her teeth.

Take the weight off her feet.

Arrest her arthritis.

Give her a blue rinse.

Iron out her wrinkles.

Banish her bunions.

Help her get dressed.

Give her a new hairdo...

and reintroduce her to your friends.

If Granny doesn't like the cold . . .

take her on a winter holiday . . .

... to sunny Spain.

If Granny complains of the damp . . .

shove her in the spin dryer . . .

and don't let her out...

until she's tumbled dry.

If Granny needs airing . . .

take her out for the day . . .

. . . to the country.

In these times of sickening crime and violence . . .

teach her self defence techniques.

Find out her phobias . . .

and cure them.

Don't let her forget...

that this is the age of the train.

JUST

FOR

FUN

Give her an exploding prune.

Put spaghetti in her spinning wheel.

Sacrifice her sewing machine.

Ask her her age.

Donate her to charity.

Put a mouse in her larder...

and feed it.

Interrupt The Archers.

Drill holes in her umbrella.

Buy her a hyperactive Venus fly trap.

Blend her budgies.

Put a bomb in her All-bran.

Give her a good book to read.

And if all else fails...

. . . tell her you're not hungry.